Salvation For?

Exploring the Human Experience of God's Saving Work

Clive Marsh

Principal, The Queen's Foundation for Ecumenical Theological Education, Birmingham, UK

GROVE BOOKS LIMITED

RIDLEY HALL RD CAMBRIDGE CB3 9HU

Contents

Acknowledgments
Thanks to James Heard and Jill Marsh for offering critical readings of draft material.

First Impression January 2021
ISSN 2633-8394
ISBN 978 1 78827 151 6

Introduction

1

What *is* salvation for? The question is easily answered. Its purpose is to bring about the best for the whole of creation. It is the action of God in and with the whole created order. It could be viewed as a restoration (of the originally good creation), or a goal (a new heaven and a new Earth). Either way, it is good news.

This booklet probes the way in which salvation actually works in human experience. Keeping the practical aspects of salvation always in view, but without reducing the doctrine of salvation to human acts or practices, it explores the 'template' of salvation. In examining how people experience salvation, and what is going on for them, it maps what it is that people are saved *from*, *for*, *by* and *into*. In the process it reveals how Christian faith, theology and practice has too often, and dangerously, been too spiritual, too individualistic and too negative in the way it has presented its key message about God. Accepting that God's salvation reaches beyond humankind (which would need a further study), this booklet looks at the human experience of God's saving work, so that the good news can be presented in all its fullness and richness.

2 Salvation in Context

'Are you saved?' For some Christians this is the key question to ask anyone, and whether one is prepared to ask the question of others becomes the hallmark of genuine faith. Behind the question lies a series of assumptions. First, salvation is being located at the centre of Christianity's reason for being. There is no purpose in church except to proclaim the message of salvation. Church then becomes the haven of the saved. Jesus' role is as redeemer, and little else. It is the death of Jesus that matters most, not the rest of his life, for it is through his death that redemption has come about. Secondly, salvation is an individual concern. The question, 'Are you saved?' is asked of the individual, who it is assumed will be aware of their situation before God and—unless they simply say, 'What do you mean?' or invite the questioner to mind their own business—can offer a positive or negative answer to the question. Thirdly by being asked in the present tense ('*Are* you saved?'), the question suggests that it is a current state or experience. 'I have salvation *now*.' Fourthly, it may be assumed that a positive response ('Yes, indeed I am saved!') results from some particular action or decision that the respondent has made. It is a conscious, cognitive step involving such a statement of faith as, 'I have chosen to believe in Jesus the redeemer by my own free choice.' Finally, it is assumed that it is known what we are being saved from.

A sense of being saved will play a central role in a person's life

So far, so simple. Even if it may seem a little old-fashioned as an approach to understanding salvation today, the framework just presented is still in active use. Whether or not it is deemed a wise kind of evangelism or faith-sharing, it still has merit. It recognizes that however one grasps the shape and content of Christian belief, a sense of being, or having been, saved will play a central role in a person's life. It acknowledges that various dimensions of Christian belief and practice—what one understands about Jesus of Nazareth, how Jesus and God are seen to be related, what the church is for, and how as individuals our lives are shaped by those factors—are all interrelated. To that extent, this quite traditional reading of salvation continues to be valuable.

This basic shape of salvation has pervaded the history of Christian spirituality. Late medieval images such as Hieronymus Bosch's *The Garden of Earthly Delights*, which on one of its panels depicts graphically the horrors of hell that await the unsaved, make it clear the awful things that it is advisable to be saved from. Portrayals of Jesus' crucifixion—in art, sculpture and more recently in film—accentuate the representative importance of his death: it was his death, but it also had more than just symbolic significance for others. 'Are you saved?' is, then, a question that still carries great weight.

But asking the question now, in the twenty-first century West, with greater knowledge than ever of the multiple contexts in which Christian faith and practice take shape around the world, gives us pause for thought. Whilst the shape of salvation implied in the question 'Are you saved?' still has value, we are faced with questions about the limited, always contextualized nature of the question and responses to it. When understood as a query about a person's ultimate well-being before God on the basis of whether or not they have made a personal (individual) decision, the enormity of the questioning is unsurprising. But there is more, much more, to be said. The particularity of the highly individualized, hell-avoiding, Western form of 'Are you saved?' needs closer scrutiny.

The particularity of 'Are you saved?' needs closer scrutiny

I am going to explore all of this further in a number of ways: by looking back beyond the Christian West, to see how Jewish ideas have fed into and continue to inform Christian understandings; by probing within and beyond Western versions of salvation in Christian practice; and by looking at the sheer comprehensibility of messages of salvation in secular societies. Above all, we shall cast a global glance at what Christianity is and does across the world. In these various ways we shall become clearer about what it means *now* to speak of salvation, as we seek to clarify what, then, is salvation *for*?

Before we dig deeper, it is worth noting a series of images which show how and why challenges to and difficulties for the doctrine of salvation emerge. What kind of salvation is being suggested by the ways in which salvation is presented? I suggest that there are five main images which can help us here: 'ark / lifeboat,' 'family / tribe / people,' 'gift,' 'health, safety and well-being' and 'lifestyle choice.' Though these are not straightforwardly biblical or traditional, and some of the phrases are not even biblical at all, they help us discern what is going on as we approach salvation as both doctrine and experience.

Working Images of Salvation

Ark / Lifeboat

An ark may be a biblical image, but a lifeboat is not. Ark can function helpfully as an image which reminds us that God is interested in rescue. The Genesis stories containing the lengthy account of the rescue of Noah and his family, and of two of each land-based animal, are well-known (Gen 6.9–9.28). God wants people to live life to the full, rather than be led astray. God wants to be identified with those of his creatures—human and animal—who have a vision of the fulfilled life for the whole of creation. 'Ark' has difficulties as an image. Less familiar are all the ramifications of the narrative: the fact that sea creatures are exempt from destruction; the difficulty of seeing God portrayed as very destructive. Children's versions of the story therefore usually focus on the rescue of the animals. The broader context—why a flood at all?—is side-stepped. Whatever is made of the full narrative in adult life, however, its pertinent points are these: God has no truck with evil; it is with the help of God that avoidance of evil occurs; a place of safety is needed for restoration and preparation for a return to healthy living.

This Jewish story remains vital as a living Christian narrative even though Christian belief and practice finds a new way—through the story of the life, death and resurrection of Jesus—to access and present God's saving activity. The key points remain consistent and continuous. The church becomes the ark—with the pluses and minuses that such an image contains. Understanding the church as the ark or as a lifeboat means that the church is engaged only and solely on a rescue mission. It is detached from the world and has no real possibility of interacting with society around it. Whilst helpful, then, in pinpointing God's concern to rescue creatures keen to work with God in promoting life, the limitation of the ark/lifeboat image is the extent of the negativity of the world (God's world) which this view of salvation implies.

Understanding the church as the ark means that it is engaged solely on a rescue mission

Family/Tribe/People

A cluster of images is needed to explore the way in which a 'saved people' are seen to be formed as a group. If we work back from 'church' as a social phenomenon we see that many images are used to try and characterize how the church as a 'redeemed community' is understood. The number of churches in the West that refer to themselves as a 'family' is striking. It is understandable why they do this, wanting a positive picture of good relations. The drawbacks are that families are not always happy and that blood ties do not necessarily mean closeness and harmony. Other images which depend on lineage are similarly problematic, even if it is clear why such images are used.

'Tribe' or 'clan' are similar to family. You are born into them, and have no say whether you belong. The ties are deep but may prove restrictive as well as offer protection. Talking of 'people' or 'a people' creates difficulties when claims are made for nations or groups of nations being (a) Christian people. The terms 'Christian nation' or 'Christendom' point to the close alliance between a religious tradition and a political structure. But the terms do not accurately characterize what it means to be a group of saved people. Christianity works with the notion of 'Israel' as a people and, following the apostle Paul, diverts the notion of being God's people to the church. Even so, belonging to a particular people is not usually thought of by Christians as itself a mark of salvation. Paul's conviction that 'Not all the offspring of Israel are truly Israel' is not just breaking open ethnic claims upon membership of God's people, but offering a challenge to any claim to be 'born into the church' (Rom 9.9). It does not work that way. Even if the church recognizes the way in which it is, or is part of, 'a chosen race, a royal priesthood, a dedicated nation, a people claimed by God for his own', it has to be very careful in how it understands this and applies it to itself (1 Pet 2.9). Belonging together is a crucial, positive element for all who count themselves amongst those being saved, but association or belonging is not by itself salvation.

Gift

A third strand of thinking about salvation relates to the image of 'gift.' The apostle Paul and those who followed his thinking in early Christianity again set the tone here. 'By grace you have been saved…by grace you have been saved through faith, and this is not your own doing; it is the gift of God' (Eph 2.5, 9). It could not be clearer. Salvation is a gift. It is not something earned, merited or bought by those who experience it. A doctrine of salvation has to do justice to this. Yet the simple question arises: why does everyone not accept the gift, or even have the gift forced upon them (for would that not be best for humanity and creation?). In addressing the question 'Yes, but what is salvation *for*?' we need to work out the actual significance of what it means to be offered a gift, and to have the right to refuse it.

Health, Safety and Well-Being

A fourth set of images relate to safety, well-being and health. In an age of safeguarding it is vital that we note the importance of this group of images. Salvation has to be recognized as to do with keeping people safe. Safeguarding is an act of safe-keeping, of prevention of harm and of the creation of safe space for flourishing. It is to do with the identification of trusting, as opposed to warped and damaging, relationships. It is wholly continuous with the thread of salvation evident in the New Testament gospels where being saved means being healed, restored, made well, brought back into healthy forms of social living. We shall need to respect and make use of Jesus' comment, 'Your faith has made you well' (*eg* Mark 5.34; 10.52). For it could also have been translated, 'Your faith has saved you.' And has the faith caused the healing? Might the apostle Paul be offended by the canonical evangelists' implication that somehow we contribute to our salvation through our choices? How do these physical healing stories relate to current understandings of what constitutes salvation? Is salvation an inner matter? Is it also a physical thing? How, if at all, do the two relate? Whatever conclusions we draw, we note the importance of salvation as relating to well-being and safety.

Lifestyle Choice

Finally, we note an unusual, and also unbiblical, image pertinent to salvation, that of lifestyle choice. It is unusual because it sounds consumerist, as if salvation is something you can take or leave. In positive terms, though, the notion of lifestyle choice signals that committing oneself to receive the gift of salvation is not simply an act of cognitive assent. You do not just agree with an idea or see salvation as the solution to a conundrum. Salvation is a life-changing commitment, affecting the whole of our life. It cannot but shape the entirety of our existence. There is, therefore, value in linking salvation to this contemporary image. That said, the element of choice has dangers, as though there might be other choices which are equally effective. And 'lifestyle' could summon up misleading images of material wealth and comfort as if salvation is linked to a particular socio-economic status. Neither of these trends would be helpful.

The Value and Limits of Images

All of these five images are starters to help us get inside some of the main features in articulating a *doctrine* of salvation, whilst respecting the *experience* of salvation. We have to straddle both aspects. We also have to be culturally engaged as we do so, otherwise the doctrine will not be communicable beyond the church. So having set a few hares running, let us dig a bit deeper.

3

From, For, By, Into: The Salvation Template

To be saved is a good thing, and a central concern of what it means to have a Christian faith and be a Christian. In mission terms, it is therefore also a good thing to commend to others. But what can we tease out of the images identified in the last chapter which help us to better understand salvation as an experience? In this chapter we shall look at what can be called a 'salvation template.' In other words, for the language of salvation to work in both theory and practice, we need to examine what a person is saved *from*, *for*, *by* and *into*. In simplest terms we shall see that Christianity, especially in the West, has been keen to emphasize what one must be saved *from*, without always spelling out as comprehensively, practically or helpfully what one is saved *for*. The practical aspects of what (or who!) does the saving, how it is achieved, and what one is saved into, have been insufficiently explored. To say that Jesus saves and that the church can be considered the redeemed community do not tell us nearly enough.

Saved For

I begin by asking what in Christian terms human beings are saved *for*. This is itself unusual because of the extent to which Christian tradition has focused so much on sin. We shall not skirt round that. But by starting the other way round, sin itself receives a different (fuller, even more real) characterization as a result.

Human beings are saved for three things. I shall develop this further later, but to summarize:

A Life with God

Irenaeus hit the nail on the head when stating that 'The glory of God is a human being fully alive' (*Against Heresies* 4.20.7). This is striking because it reverses what one might expect—God being glorified in and through God's creatures. It indicates how committed God is to the material realm. We might even call this the fullest expression of incarnation. If God is glorified through fully living human beings, then fully human beings are what God is committed to. The purpose of salvation is nothing other than enabling human beings to be located within the life of God. Some kind of direct, constructive association with God and / or participation in God is what salvation means for humanity. It is the basis for exploring what salvation means in practice.

A Flourishing, Fulfilled Life

The kind of life that results from such association with God needs some unpacking. We can characterize it as a flourishing, fulfilled life. As a life with and / or within God, such a life is already enjoyed now and continues, as God wills, beyond our present life. Without seeking either to address or resolve questions about what occurs beyond our physical death, we are to begin to enjoy what it means to be a saved, or being saved, person in this life. We already *have* redemption in some sense (Rom 5.1). It is not wholly about what is anticipated in the future, even if more is in store. Such a life of flourishing is therefore clearly to be participated in and enjoyed in *this present* world, whatever our circumstances. Instantly, the notion of flourishing as both something to be enjoyed *here and now* also becomes a challenge to any over-individualized notion of salvation whereby a saved person becomes concerned solely with their own salvation regardless of what happens to anyone else. For if the circumstances of a sister or brother are such that a flourishing life is less feasible for them, then it becomes my concern too. This will become a prominent aspect of our grasp of what we need to be saved *from* and *into*.

The Kingdom/Realm of God

In keeping with how Jesus is portrayed in the gospels—especially Matthew, Mark and Luke—those who follow Jesus and claim him to be (the) Christ recognize that the kingdom, or realm, of God is the heart of Christian belief and practice. If there is any talk of salvation, and any sense that Jesus' activity in the past and God's continuing presence and action in Christ are to take shape in a person's life, then it will be as a person acknowledges their place within the kingdom of God. To be a saved person means to be positioned within the realm of God's reign. This affects how an individual thinks and behaves and cannot be confined just to what an individual says or does. Being saved *for* life within God's reign means clarifying, as will be noted shortly, what one is saved *into*, for it is clear from the gospels that there is an irreducibly social, communal aspect to God's kingdom. Similarly, there is an irreducibly social and communal dimension to what it means to be a saved person.

Saved By

By what, or whom, are people saved? By God, obviously. But Christians have been much more specific. With the conviction that God was doing something particular and special in and through the life, death and resurrection of Jesus, the whole question about *how* God saved and saves took on a fresh turn. Within this particular moment of salvation much Christianity has focused upon the death of Jesus as a point in history—*the* point in history—when salvation was achieved. There is no denying this crucial element of the drama of salvation. Whatever is made of the person of Jesus, within and beyond Christianity, some understanding has to be offered of his violent death. But a contemporary Christian's link with Jesus the Christ is not simply based on a reference to a past event. The ongoing human experience of connectedness with Christ contains a link back to a significant point in past history *and* refers to participation in the ongoing life which God has enabled in and through the person of Jesus the Christ. We are saved by God in Jesus Christ. That means we have to associate ourselves with the past figure who was crucified and whom the earliest followers claimed was raised from death. We do not have to agree as Christians what exactly happened as a result of Jesus' death. Nor do we have to agree in precise terms what the resurrection means. We do, though, have to be committed to the God whose self-giving for the world we see embodied in the person of Jesus. If God was, as Paul says, in Christ reconciling the world to Godself, then it is not our actions which save us (2 Cor 5.19). However we understand the meaning of Jesus' death, it is God's self-giving which enables us to participate in God's saving work.

Let us face it: too much ink has been spilt on clarifying exactly how Jesus' death as an atoning sacrifice is best understood (propitiation? expiation? exemplar?). The very discussion raises questions about the adequacy, and morality, of doctrines of God. For why would God require such a sacrifice? If, though, we begin at the other end in exploring salvation (what are we saved *for*?) and work back, then different nuances of how to understand Jesus' death become less relevant.

The violent death of Jesus cannot be dodged

Again, let us be clear: the violent death of Jesus cannot be dodged. Those who participate in God's saving work are saved by a God who takes risks. Jesus risked death, acting, as divine Son, in obedience to God the Father. Jesus' followers take similar risks. But by being committed to the God embodied in Jesus Christ, whose death was in some clear sense not the end, then those participating in salvation are saved by God in and through Jesus Christ for a life of flourishing and into a hopeful future.

The Presence of Jesus

'Being saved by' therefore also needs an ongoing, present dimension to it. For if the full story of how and by whom we are saved is not contained simply in the reference back to the death of Jesus, then it has to be shown how those who participate in God's saving activity continue to relate to Jesus the Christ. Christianity does this in a number of ways, in both theory and practice. Followers of Jesus are 'in Christ' (see, for example, Rom 12.5; 16.7; 1 Cor 4.15; 15.19; 2 Cor 1.21; 5.17; 12.2; Gal 3.28). The link to Jesus the historical figure is more than a memory. When Christians say 'Jesus is here,' they do not mean that a first-century Palestinian has walked into the room. They are referring to the nature of the presence of God in the present, and to the fact that that presence is Christlike, and continuous with the life, death and resurrection of Jesus.[1]

'In Christ' language also connects with 'body of Christ' language (Rom 12.5; 1 Cor 12.27). The apostle Paul used both ways of speaking in pointing out the communal dimension of Christian experience and the emotional intensity and deeply collaborative nature of participation in God's saving work. Because of this, it is understandable why Christians call the church 'the body of Christ' ('...you *are* the body of Christ,' 1 Cor 12.27, my emphasis). The tricky thing is that if we work back from churches as we know them now, then we may miss some key aspects of what Paul is getting at. Bearing in mind that early Christians were forming new kinds of groups, in a mission context, and often in quite beleaguered settings where many experienced persecution, then we may lose sight of the intensity and person-forming character of those early Christian communities. We now need to pay attention to other communal groups (*eg* political, community, health and well-being, educational) which prove formative and transformative in order to identify how and where God's saving action in Christ is perceptible today.[2] We shall develop this further below when asking what people are saved into.

Through the Spirit

A further way in which Christians speak of God's continuing presence is as, and through, the Holy Spirit. The Spirit denotes a specific way in which God is, and acts as, God. The Spirit is the Spirit of Christ, and therefore we can detect where God's Spirit is at work by looking for Christlike actions and presence. Strikingly, even though God's Spirit is present in a Christlike way, this pneumatological insight provides space for noting how God is active in ways that break out of narrowly Christian moulds. It is not accidental that those engaged in interfaith dialogue find that 'Spirit talk' is sometimes easier to handle than 'Christ talk.' Such Spirit talk is no less Christian. For Christians, though, the in-Christness of Christian perception shapes what they say when they see God's Spirit at work.

To say that people are saved by God in Jesus means that we have to expand the moment of Jesus' life, death and resurrection to grasp what is going on: God's self-giving in Christ does not end with Jesus's death. It continues in multiple forms. Those multiple forms (being in Christ, church, intense communal experiences, spiritual presence, interfaith encounter) are wide-ranging but profound. They are the participative contexts in which salvation is experienced. As such they are also the settings which people are saved into.

Saved Into

A saved person is not abandoned to a solitary life. God acted *in the past* in Jesus, and that was a decisive saving act. Yet the way in which an ongoing relationship with Christ takes shape *in the present* has to be expressed. And if a strong *future* sense of salvation is held, according to which salvation is deemed to come to fruition at the end of time rather than now, there is still a need to recognize how salvation may be experienced here and now *with others* in anticipation of God's future. It is therefore important to clarify how salvation is experienced and enjoyed communally. However salvation is understood, the flourishing life which a person is saved *for* is not merely an individual or individualistic experience. How could it be? In the same way that it is not good for anyone to be alone, so also it is recognized that salvation has a communal dimension to it (Gen 2.18). How, then, is salvation in Christ actually experienced communally, particularly in forms other than church? In what ways is church a helpful and unhelpful way of characterizing what it means to be a saved person?

People are saved for the kingdom of God

People are saved *for* the kingdom/realm of God. This is the overarching context within which we are to understand and experience what Christians are saved *into*. The kingdom of God is an arena within which God is active, and this is perceived by those open to the salvation which God brings. It is not an exclusively Christian concept or practice, for God's will and actions may be evident in many different areas of life. Nor do people bring the kingdom about. All we can do is work in such a way that we assist God in the creation of conditions in which the kingdom may come and be received as a gift. If we do not exercise this degree of reserve, then we are seeking to take the place of God.

For Christians, the lens of Christlikeness enables perception of where and how God's kingdom breaks in. God's realm is not, however, to be identified precisely with any particular human structure, community or organization. No church, no community group, no political party can embody the kingdom of God. They can only serve the kingdom as they seek to participate in it.

People are thus saved into fallible, frail, limited, incomplete, messy human structures. Those who as individuals believe that God saves, and who open themselves up to receiving the joys and benefits of God's grace, remain flawed human beings, even as they are being saved by God. In the same way, the communal contexts within which individuals perceive and participate in God's kingdom-related action are also flawed. Social sin is as significant as the sin with which individuals have to wrestle. Recognizing that we have to face these realities full on brings us, finally, to the question with which Christian accounts of salvation very often begin: what is it that we are saved *from*?

Saved From

I place the question of what people are saved *from* last quite deliberately. Even though there is a quick, shorthand answer to the question—sin!—there has been an overemphasis upon it in much Christian history and practice.[3] Whilst such overemphasis is understandable, for sin is real and nasty, this does not always help pastorally or missiologically. Yet it is vital, in exploring doctrine, to think pastorally and in terms of mission. Conversely, those engaged in pastoral, evangelistic and missionary practice must also think and behave in a doctrinally informed way. To put it another way, there is no point making people feel bad about themselves to start with in order to show the good things God has provided or can do. Successful, confident people might well have uncomfortable things they need to discover about themselves, but it is not going to help to try and drag them down first. Others who might be carrying all sorts of hurt and guilt, or who wrestle with low self-esteem or depression, are not going to be helped by being brought even lower. The good news of the gospel will ultimately always be positive. But it connects with people—and discloses to them—in different ways what it is that people need saving from, even if 'sin' proves a catch-all term.

Sin is the distortion and disruption of creation's, and therefore also human beings,' relationship to God. It is a consequence of the freedom granted to the created order. It affects the individual human being in so far as everyone at some stage is faced with the full reality of their own freedom, and realizes that although created good, and for goodness, they do not *have* to do good, act justly or consider others. And every human being in some way practises the alternative to the good and wise option. ('...All have sinned and fall short of the glory of God' [Rom 3.23].) For to be fully focused on God—*ie* being in tune with the creator and the creator's will and purpose for the universe—would mean acting justly and considerately all the time. But because everyone does act sinfully it seems as though we are wired to be sinful, like a disease that grips us. For that is how it feels. ('I do not understand my own actions. For I do not do what I want, but I do the very thing I hate' [Rom 7.15].) What saves us, though, is not simply a matter of choosing *not* to sin, as if it were a straightforward issue of moral choice. Being saved is about being reoriented by and towards God.

We can only face our sin with God's help

Christian doctrine hinges, then, on the doctrine of salvation. All other doctrinal themes serve the task of spelling out what it means for the created order to be released from sin. We can, though, only grasp what sin is and how it gets dealt with from the perspective, and in the knowledge, of what God has done and is doing in Christ. We can only face our sin with God's help. The consequences of our sin upon us and the world can only be expunged by God's work upon and within us. In exploring and presenting what we are saved *for,* we work back from the knowledge God gives, and the actions God has taken and takes in Christ, to see what we are saved *from*. How, though, are such matters going to be heard in contemporary culture? And what more can be said about how what we are saved *for* affects daily practice? These questions are addressed in the remaining chapters.

4 Salvation and Contemporary Culture

Where do these contemporary reflections on an old theme leave us? Even accepting that salvation might be mapped as a framework of what one is saved from, for, by and into, where does it fit in now, especially in trying to make doctrine comprehensible in broader society? Even if what one is saved *for* is accentuated more than in the past, how is that going to help? How and why is this particular take on salvation of use in the present, and how can we be sure it remains faithful to the Christian tradition even as it adopts a distinctly contemporary form?

In this chapter we look briefly at ways in which salvation language persists in everyday speech and cultural life, whether or not it is specifically acknowledged as religious language. Without assuming or concluding that any and every use of words such as salvation, save, liberation, redemption or rescue carry explicitly theological overtones, it is vital that we explore how these words appear in society. For without connecting theological uses of salvation with where similar terms appear it may not be possible to speak to our generation easily about matters of faith.

In *A Cultural Theology of Salvation*, I presented a range of examples of where redemption language appears in the media and broader culture.[4] To those examples many more can be added. You could find your own examples with the briefest of Google searches. In my own case I came across two feature films bearing the simple title *Redemption* within the past decade. In sport, redemption stories abound. Examples from boxing, golf, cricket, basketball and football were easy to locate, though the experience of the American football star Michael Vick, as reported by Guy Giles, is telling: 'Sporting redemption is one thing, but redemption in the real world is something entirely different.'[5]

Key things to note from any rapid trawl through contemporary media and popular culture are:

- that common usage picks up on the fact that major change occurs in a person's life; and
- that change is a recovery of some kind, a rescue, a making good in response to something troubling in the past.

In these respects, the notion of redemption as a form of salvation acknowledges that people are saved *from* something (past failure, a sense of guilt, a burden they are carrying) *for* something fresh and invigorating (*eg* the exhilaration of new success).

There are also features that, in some cases, articulate the hopes and aspirations of salvation's reach:

- that some deep, emotional stuff often has to be dealt with when salvation takes effect; and
- that it is, potentially at least, *for all*, and thus for lots of different types of people, and not exclusively for any kind of in-group.

Elements of what a *theological* approach to salvation enables us to explore further, beyond mentions of redemption in everyday speech, comprise the recognition that:

- we cannot save or redeem ourselves (it just is not that simple);
- it is not a matter of just trying a bit harder;
- salvation is perhaps not to be viewed in terms of success at all; and
- it will include attention to forgiving self-acceptance.

Theology cannot simply read off from such experiences an exposition of a theological understanding of redemption, nor assume that there is no link at all. If sporting redemption is not the same as redemption in the real world, investigation into what salvation can mean in a fuller sense is invited.[6] It is also welcome to recognize that theology and faith are seeking to demonstrate what it means to live in the (really) real world!

Christian theological thought is not to be wholly negative, then, about what may be considered worldly understandings of salvation. In interacting with descriptions of human experience of failure, fragility, loss, brokenness and inadequacy, theology invites reflection from the perspective of its narratives about a God who is always present and able to accompany people through a process of restoration and recovery to a new, more hopeful place. Christian insights are relevant to, and offer contributions to understanding of, human experiences where God may not happen to be named. For all forms of forgiveness, all forms of honest self-discovery, all types of transformation into a direction of hopeful, healthy living can be argued to have God as their source.

In still more focused Christian terms, it is the life, death and resurrection of Jesus and the ensuing experience of the community that continues to bear witness to Jesus (the church in all its rich, global diversity) which enable experiences of salvation to be identified, interpreted and narrated. This chapter suggests that to attempt to express doctrinal claims in solely internal theological (or church) terms without acknowledging the linguistic complexity of the world we live in could be misleading, even dangerous. This observation accentuates the missiological dimension to doctrine. If we are going to have a chance of communicating anything about faith, then we must think carefully about the language we use. This does not mean that the content of doctrine is being *controlled* by the wider world, even if it is *influenced* by it. In other words, the contexts in which doctrine is articulated have to be examined closely by those who express faith, and not simply so that it is clear what kind of world a doctrine is being launched into. This would imply that Christians are learning nothing from God through the world in which we believe God to be present and active (*ie* beyond the church). Context matters with respect to the content of doctrine, without either determining what is to be said of God or being insignificant.

It is for this reason that it is important to explore the concept of happiness with respect to salvation. Happiness is unlikely to prove satisfactory as an exhaustive definition for, or means of clarifying fully, what salvation is for. However, it is beyond doubt a contemporary frame of reference for helping Western citizens (and potentially people across the world) to explore the doctrine of salvation. As we shall see in the final chapter, the multiple potential meanings of happiness correlate well with some.of the range of meanings of salvation. In the same way that redemption can be sold short in everyday speech, so also happiness can be defined quite superficially. Without concluding too easily that only Christians know what true happiness really is, the contemporary exploration of what salvation is *for* can also help theology and faith connect and contribute to current understandings of what life is about.

5

Salvation 'For,' Once More

To focus on what salvation is *for* runs the risk of pandering to a consumerist age. A concern to clarify what the benefits of salvation are, could so easily become a 'What's in it for me?' approach. Not only might salvation become self-interested, it could also be highly individualistic. Whilst wanting to avoid an overemphasis on what we are saved *from*, switching to focus on what we are saved *for* could raise a new set of problems. The content of this chapter has to be understood in the light of the template considered in chapter three. In spelling out how salvation is about fulfilment—of the whole of creation, not just human beings—and in this present life, not just beyond physical death, we cannot overlook the other three elements. None of what we perceive salvation to be for would be possible without the framework of God's action, in Christ, combatting sin in individual and social forms, bringing us into rich forms of human community. This is not just background or preamble. It is the context within which salvation works. But we are also trying to articulate the good news which theology seeks to present, bearing in mind the context and constraints identified in chapter four: redemption language might be well-used, and happiness might be fashionable, but what, if anything, do they have to do with salvation?

I have expounded more fully what salvation amounts to in practice in my longer study.[7] Here I offer a succinct, abbreviated statement of what salvation is.

Salvation is about life, full life, abundant life, fulfilling life

Salvation is about *life, full life, abundant life, fulfilling life* (John 10.10; 20.31). The resurrecting God signals a commitment to opposing death in all its forms by raising Jesus from the dead. Affirmation of God's resurrecting activity means participating in God's persistent, continuing, energetic drive for life through the whole of creation. This is what we are called to choose (Deut 30.19).

This does not, though, mean any kind of life. The language of eternal life can prove misleading if it is thought that merely having one's life extended interminably is a good thing. For it is often true that towards the end of their biological life people feel that they have had enough and are ready to go. Eternal life needs to be understood as life with God. We are talking about a quality of a particular kind of life. In so far as we recognize that our lives are short and limited in scope in comparison to eternity, then it is inevitable that we look to God for any kind of life with God beyond physical death. To say that salvation is about life means entrusting to God our well-being, whatever steps we may have taken to live well.

Another way of saying what salvation is for, then, is *ultimate well-being*. It is ultimate because, as a gift from God, salvation takes us beyond whatever forms of well-being we aspire to, or enjoy, in the present. However we may understand well-being now, the fact that salvation results in life with God means more than whatever efforts we make to keep ourselves fit, maintain our work-life balance or emotional stability, or uphold our mental health. These are all crucial things for human beings to be doing, and dovetail with any spiritual or religious practices we undertake. But they do not of themselves produce ultimate well-being. Salvation is not to be equated with health (physical, spiritual, mental, emotional) though all of these forms of health are connected to it. The frailty and fragility of life means that we know ultimate well-being is not experienced fully in this life, even if it may be glimpsed. Human experience includes a vast range of different aspects of physical, mental and emotional well-being. Accepting, coping with and—where possible—addressing these aspects becomes a feature of spiritual life, undertaken within the framework of God's saving activity.

Salvation has to do with freedom, or liberation

Salvation involves *release*. This is the positive flip side of the attention paid in the history of Christian thought and practice to sin. Salvation has to do with freedom, or liberation. However, there are different ways of understanding the freedom experienced. For there are inner aspects (emotional, mental, cognitive) and sociopolitical dimensions (relating to material and communal well-being). These different aspects interweave. At root is the removal of whatever obstacles block the flourishing of the individual human being, of humanity and of the whole created order. God's saving activity removes barriers, restores wholeness, reconciles where there is discord and hostility, and nourishes where there is lack. However, the God-given freedom which creation enjoys does not automatically lead to release, freedom or liberation. Humanity in particular contributes to obstacle-building through multiple unjust and hostile practices (war, structures of inequality, slavery, oppressive working practices, crime and violence). The doctrine of salvation therefore explicates the *offer* of release, and signals the *capacity* of God to save, together with a mapping of how human beings may participate in this desire of God for the world. Sin remains very real within this drama. Human opposition to the free gifts God makes available is real too.

Salvation has to do with *safety*. One of the dominant motifs throughout the Jewish and Christian traditions is the search for a safe place to be. The riskiness of life is not to be avoided, and has to be acknowledged and faced head on. Yet God seeks both to bring people to safety, and to be with those who have gathered together in search of safety. It is no accident that there are many images in the Bible and in Jewish and Christian history of this quest for sanctuary, for a haven, a place of peace. Nor is it coincidental that the primary meaning of sanctuary as a holy place (a temple or church) should now carry an additional meaning, used in multiple ways with a political resonance in relation to the plight of asylum seekers and refugees, of being a place free from harm or persecution. There are many other concrete examples to note: youth workers seeking to create safe spaces for young people to be themselves and to discover or explore their identity; social and community workers working alongside women who have suffered domestic violence arranging places in safe houses; social and political concern for the safeguarding of children and vulnerable adults; churches which may themselves be considered havens. These are all images of human activity which pertain to salvation. They are variants on the ark or lifeboat image introduced in chapter two. When understood in the light of being holy places and places of peace (spaces where God is), their link with the saving work of God becomes clear. In specifically Christian terms, God is seen to bring peace in the risen Christ (John 20.21, 26).

Salvation has *forgiveness* at its core. To be in relationship with God means recognizing that God is the source of all forgiveness. God enables us to acknowledge and face the flaws and shortcomings in ourselves, and the impact that these have on the way we relate to others. God is also able to absorb and deal with the consequences of those shortcomings. However individual Christians may understand the meanings and significance of the crucifixion of Jesus, it has become a focal point for understanding God's self-giving. The cross, understood both in itself and in light of the resurrection, helps us grasp the way in which we may participate in the forgiveness that God offers—and seeks to enact—in and through our own forgiving, reconciling relationships ('And forgive us our sins, for we ourselves forgive everyone indebted to us…' [Luke 11.4]). The Lord's Prayer is a reminder that prayer is not just words but a life-shaping practice. To be a being-saved person is to endeavour to be a forgiving person who has accepted the fact that they are accepted by God.[8]

Salvation has forgiveness at its core

Salvation entails *communal celebration.* I recall hearing more than once in my youth the phrase, 'No-one gets into heaven on anyone else's coat-tails.' I always thought it an odd, quaint turn of phrase. With hindsight it strikes me now as deeply individualistic. Yet it also contains a simple, existential truth: receiving the salvation God offers really is a personal, individual matter. Salvation may, though, hinge less on conscious individual decision than the remembered quotation from my youth suggests: individual openness, yes; dependence on individual decision *alone*, certainly not. For individual salvation is bound up with belonging to a people of the kingdom. It is enjoyed as a response to what has been offered, and to what has been—and is being—carried by a group: as a message, as a practice, as a lived experience. It is celebrated ritually by Christians of all traditions, whatever different denominations say about their willingness to accept the ritualistic nature of their own practice! Mass / eucharist / holy communion / Lord's supper / breaking of bread are different names for a celebration which most Christians participate in to mark the communal dimension of salvation. Other practices (hymn singing, public prayer, liturgical chanting, praise worship) accentuate the fact that salvation is a communal, as well as an individual reality. They consolidate the extent to which salvation is participated in—as opposed simply to being claimed for oneself—and is to be celebrated as a thing of joy.

Finally, salvation produces *contentment*. I use this word advisedly, as opposed to happiness, although salvation is entangled with happiness through being bound up with joy. If being saved by God is not a matter of joy, then something has gone amiss. Salvation does not, though, inevitably make a person happy in a consistent, straightforward sense. To struggle with constant back pain, to live with deep grief, to feel persistent anxiety, are all examples of life situations which may prevent a person feeling happy in a sense of having lasting emotional satisfaction. Yet such people can also be amongst those who are being saved. The happiness that may come can be a sense of deep contentment which rests less on their own physical situation or feelings, and more on the inner sense of well-being they experience (a settled emotional state, we might say). Contentment may come best from connectedness with others, whether this is a physical presence with others, or a consciousness of relationship with people present or past. The communion of saints—that awareness of being with others who throughout history have known the gracious activity of God—is an emotionally powerful, and not just a symbolic, reality. This kind of contentment may also be called blessedness: a state which moves beyond what we may feel or experience subjectively, for ourselves, and involves acknowledging that it is God that enables our contented state to come about. We are blessed in the sense of experiencing the well-being which the knowledge of being saved produces.

Salvation does not inevitably make a person happy

And here we have come full circle: the blessedness which God brings, and which we feel, *is* the full, abundant life that salvation is for, the ultimate well-being provided potentially for the whole of creation. It is that for which creation longs and groans, not yet fully realized, but glimpsed and grasped in part (Rom 8.22). The distance between the already (the kingdom here) and the not yet (the kingdom yet to come) makes us ache with longing. But in giving thanks for the present, and awaiting what God still has in store for the world, we are also already joyfully content. Salvation is for *now*, and for the future.

6 Salvation in Practice

Where does all this lead? How is a doctrine of salvation to be lived? In this concluding chapter I offer brief insights into what salvation means for everyday life.

Recognizing Limitations

The doctrine of salvation encourages us to face up to who we really are. It is sad that for so much of Christian history this aspect of the doctrine has been received as being a negative thing ('You are a bad person') when it is about facing facts. I get fed up when I hear successful people say something like, 'I am proof that you can be anything you want to be if you just try hard enough.' If it is a TV or online interview I am watching, then I want to shout, 'No, you can't!' If you are 5′ 3″ (1.60m) tall then you are not going to be a world-record-holding high jumper. Accepting how things really are about ourselves takes us well beyond just respecting our limitations, whilst including that. Even God cannot help us if we refuse to acknowledge honestly who we are, and what we can and cannot do.

Facing Honestly Our Own, Others' and Social Evils

Sin is relevant here, though may not be the best way, culturally, of talking about the reality of evil. But we do have to find a way of identifying and talking about any propensity to be self-centred and to deceive, mislead, even abuse others. We also have to add to individual issues the fact of social evil: the ways in which we are all entangled, in society and in communities of which we are part, in murky goings-on. We cannot flourish whilst all such tendencies hold sway, even though we know that we continue to struggle against such tendencies even as God is helping (saving) us.

Living within Appropriate Boundaries

This is another way of saying, 'Whom do you trust?' Or we could ask, 'Amongst whom do we expect to grow, as people?' We are also trying to identify here the people amongst whom we can be most ourselves, utterly honestly, the ones who will ask hard and tough questions of us when we act unreasonably, disrespectfully or in ways which damage others. It would be nice to think that the community called church might be such a body of people. We must also recognize that churches aspire to be, though do not always succeed in being, safe communities: places within which people can be wholly themselves, warts and all, precisely because they are communities within which the forgiveness of God is acknowledged and received, and the freedom is granted to re-enter the wider world as renewed people. Religions are only boundaried so that they enable people to grow within them. They become stifling when they do not function as channels for enabling God to work on and with people *for* their living in the world.

Structuring Daily Life

And daily life? This heading and the next show us two aspects of how the constant awareness of being a saved person takes shape in practice. A fulfilled and flourishing life is not a collection of emotional highs. Sometimes the thirst for transcendence becomes a quest for transcendent moments, spiritual kicks, whether gained through worship, surfing, rock concerts or walks in the country. In reality, salvation is usually experienced and enjoyed in more mundane ways. It is important to recall daily what it means to be a person who is always conscious of benefiting from the gracious presence of a loving God in one's life. Salvation consciousness shapes our being to the very core. Bringing our saved state to mind, then, can be a daily discipline, informing how we behave.

Knowing How Best to Treat People

Salvation consciousness goes beyond what we do as individuals. Because we are shaped as people by our sense of what we are saved from, for and into, and by whom we are saved, our whole conduct is affected. Radical self-awareness—of our own flaws and potential for evil, and our own need of grace—gives us insight into others and how we treat other people. Knowing that all human beings are sinful and in need of saving grace enables the cultivation of realism in human relationships and sensitivity in handling the shortcomings of others. We are also invited to think of how hope may get a look-in at every turn. Knowing that Jesus Christ died for all means respecting the fact that the lavish forgiveness and saving grace of God is available to everyone we meet.

On Living Interdependently

Salvation's social aspect takes us beyond the individual. Attention to who and what we are saved *into* urges us to focus on communities and groups which enable people to flourish. Social sin needs to be identified and addressed. Salvation in social form is the kingdom breaking in, whatever form that takes. Christians will not only form churches in order to anticipate the kingdom's coming. They will celebrate where God's kingdom is evident in other faith traditions, in politics, in community life. Christians who explicitly speak of God's saving work in Christ will use their knowledge of Jesus Christ to detect the presence and activity of God wherever it is evident. In doing so they recognize that God speaks and acts in in-between spaces, between Christians, between Christians and others, between humanity and the rest of creation. If salvation is about the ultimate flourishing of the whole created order, then it entails God's drawing all into harmonious interrelating despite the awfulness of what humanity can sometimes do, and of what can occur naturally within the world.

A Final Reflection

We shall not be able to know for sure this side of our own physical deaths whether the drama of salvation we have explored is 'just a story.' Calling it just a story, though, is unhelpful anyway, because as a story it forms a template which shapes actual life. Like all the best narratives in and through which we work out how best to live with and within nature and with each other, the Christian account of salvation presents itself, then, as more than just a story. It proves accurate, telling, informative and deeply life-shaping, and thereby offers itself also as both truthful and true.

Notes

1 C Marsh, *Christ in Practice: A Christology of Everyday Life* (London: Darton, Longman and Todd, 2006) chs 1-2.

2 *Christ in Practice, op cit*, chs 3-6.

3 I would also suggest that an overemphasis on any one of the four elements of the template leads to major distortion of Christian thought and practice.

4 Specific media examples are cited in *A Cultural Theology of Salvation* (Oxford University Press, 2018) pp 13-15. Part two of the work then looks at the way the theme of salvation/redemption surfaces in all sorts of ways within culture past and present (pp 59-158).

5 G Giles, '5 of the greatest sporting redemption stories,' 24 Feb 2020 (accessed 22 April 2020).

6 I hesitate to say 'really means,' as salvation really means all sorts of things to different people. But our task as a church is to enter cultural discussions and experiences and invite reflection on what theological understandings contribute to understandings of reality and of well-being, human and otherwise.

7 C Marsh, *A Cultural Theology of Salvation* (Oxford University Press, 2018) esp pp 187-228.

8 I am echoing here the strikingly simple yet beautiful formulation of Paul Tillich: 'Simply accept the fact that you are accepted!' P Tillich, *The Shaking of the Foundations* (New York: Charles Scribner's Sons, 1948) p 162.